Great BIG Dinosaur

Written by Myka-Lynne Sokoloff

Celebration Press
Parsippany, New Jersey

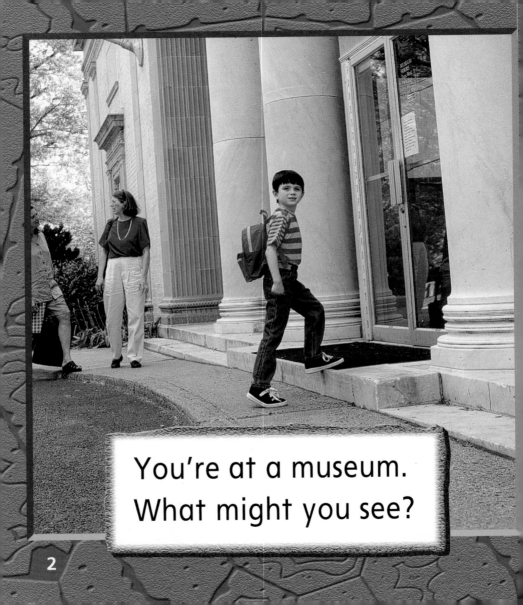

You're at a museum.
What might you see?

Let's take a look.
What could it be?

You see a great big head
and great big teeth.

You see great big toes
and great big feet.

You see a great big tail . . .

and even more . . .

You see a great big dinosaur!